ANIMAL ALBUMS

THE HORSE FAMILY

BY GOLRIZ GOLKAR

eureka!

EUREKA!, AN IMPRINT OF BELLWETHER MEDIA BY FLUTTERBEE

eureka!

Eureka! books turn real stories into unforgettable experiences. Clear, direct language and sharp, captivating imagery make it easy to follow your curiosity, one fascinating fact at a time. Your Eureka! moment awaits!

This edition first published in 2027 by Bellwether Media, Inc.

For information regarding permission, write to Bellwether Media, Inc., Attention: Permissions Department, 3500 American Blvd W, Suite 150, Bloomington, MN 55431.

Library of Congress Cataloging-in-Publication Data is available at www.loc.gov or upon request from the publisher.

ISBN: 9798898801311 (hardcover)
ISBN: 9798898802554 (ebook)

Editor: Rebecca Sabelko Series Designer: Jeff Kollock

Printed in the United States of America, North Mankato, MN.

TABLE OF CONTENTS

WHAT ARE EQUINES?

Equines are mammals of the Equidae family. This includes more than 400 horse breeds, three zebra species, and three ass, or donkey, species. Equines live on every continent except Antarctica. Domestic horses and some donkeys live on farms and ranches. Other equines live in the wild. Most male equines are called stallions. Most females are called mares. Male donkeys are jacks, and female donkeys are jennets.

▲ HORSE

▲ DONKEY

▼ MOUNTAIN ZEBRA

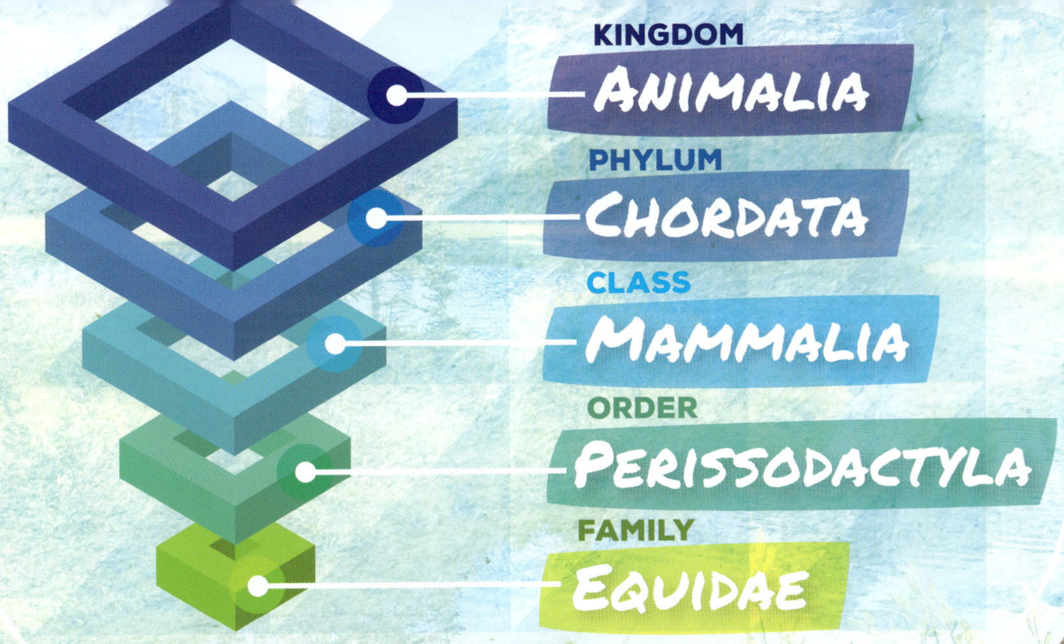

TAXONOMY CHART

Equines have furry manes. Many have long tails. They are strong animals with four powerful legs. Each foot has a single toe protected by a thick hoof.

PACK MULES ▲
carrying supplies

KINDS OF HORSES

Draft horses are bred to pull heavy loads. Light horses are bred for riding and sports. Ponies are among the smallest breeds. They are used for driving, riding, and carrying objects.

THE HISTORY OF EQUINES

Equids first appeared around 55 million years ago in North America. These small animals lived in subtropical forests and ate soft plants. North America became drier as Earth's climate cooled. Equids adapted to living in grassland habitats. New species grew larger. Their legs became longer. They developed teeth for grinding tough grasses.

▲ **EOHIPPUS**
earliest equid

DISAPPEARING HORSES

Around 10,000 years ago, horses had disappeared from North America. They may have struggled to adapt to the changing climate. They may have become food for humans. Spanish colonizers brought horses back to North America in the 1500s.

MESOHIPPU ▼
early equine ancestor

CAVE PAINTING ▲
of early domestication

Ancestors of modern horses developed around 4.5 million years ago in North America. These animals, called *Equus*, eventually migrated into Asia and spread into Europe and Africa. *Equus* evolved into horses, zebras, and donkeys about two million years ago. Humans domesticated horses around 4,000 years ago.

EVOLUTIONARY EXCELLENCE

LIFE CYCLE

Equines give birth to live babies called foals. Domestic mares often give birth to a single foal about 11 months after mating. Most give birth every other year. Foals run just a few hours after they are born. They rely on grains and their mother's milk for several months. Then they begin eating grass. Domestic foals often stay with their mothers until around six months old. Most equines reach adulthood around the age of five.

▲ FOALS

GRAINS ▶

Humans breed domestic horses. They breed horses for specific traits such as speed and pulling strength.

EQUINE LANGUAGE AND BEHAVIOR

SHARP SENSES

Equines have good hearing and vision. Their sharp sight and smell help them remember people and places.

BODY LANGUAGE

Equines let their ears fall to the sides and their tails hang when they are calm. They show their teeth and press their ears back to show frustration. Equines run away from danger. They kick in defense. Horses often show the whites of their eyes when they are afraid.

SOUNDS

Horses whinny to find one another. Donkeys and zebras bray when they are excited or to warn of danger. Horses nicker to attract mates, ask for food, and communicate with foals.

ZEBRAS ▲
braying

EQUINE FAMILY TREE

DOMESTIC HORSES

▲ **SHIRE HORSES**

Shire horses are the largest horse breed in the world.

▲ **THOROUGHBRED HORSES**

▲ **AMERICAN QUARTER HORSES**

American quarter horses help ranchers round up cattle. They can sense how cows will behave.

WILD AND FERAL HORSES

▲ **PRZEWALSKI'S HORSES**

Cave paintings in Europe from around 25,000 years ago show the stocky features of this horse.

▲ **AMERICAN MUSTANG HORSES**

EQUIDAE

PONIES

▲SHETLAND PONIES

▲CONNEMARA PONIES

ZEBRAS

No two zebras have the same stripe pattern. Zebras may be able to recognize one another by their stripe patterns.

ASSES

▲DONKEYS

EQUINE BIOGRAPHIES LIPIZZAN HORSES

Lipizzans have Spanish, Arabian, and Berber roots. They were brought to Lipizza in modern-day Slovenia in the 1500s. They were bred as royal horses.

ORIGIN MAP

SKILLS AND TRAITS

Lipizzans are friendly, athletic, graceful, and focused. They are used for carriage driving, riding, and dressage. They are famous for performing highly skilled routines. These include difficult jumps and balances.

APPEARANCE

These horses are compact but strong. Their heads are narrow. Their chests are wide and deep. Foals are born with dark coats. Many begin to turn white to light gray around age four. Some remain dark as adults.

FAMOUS LIPIZZANS

LIPIZZAN HORSES OF THE SPANISH RIDING SCHOOL

- **Location:**
  Vienna, Austria
- **Famous for:**
  Lipizzan stallions live, train, and perform at this school. They put on a skilled show set to classical music. It is called the *Ballet of the White Stallions*.

HEIGHT COMPARISON

40IN (102 cm)	60IN (152 cm)	64IN (163 cm)
Shetland pony	Arabian horse	Lipizzan horse

ARABIAN HORSES

Arabian horses are one of the oldest breeds in the world. They were first bred on the Arabian Peninsula around 5,000 years ago.

APPEARANCE

Arabian horses are slim and compact with small, wedge-shaped heads. They have short backs with sloping shoulders and strong hind legs. They may be gray, black, light brown, or reddish brown.

HEIGHT COMPARISON

ARABIAN ROOTS

Most light horse breeds today are descended from Arabian horses.

ORIGIN MAP

FAMOUS ARABIAN

MARENGO

- **Locations:**
  Egypt, France, England

- **Famous for:**
  Marengo was the French emperor Napoleon Bonaparte's horse from around 1800 to 1815. His skeleton is on display at the National Army Museum in London.

SKILLS AND TRAITS

These light horses are gentle, intelligent, and fast. Their endurance allows them to compete in 100-mile (161-kilometer) races. Arabians can handle rough terrain and strong heat. They are used for everyday riding, dressage, and ranch work.

THOROUGHBRED HORSES

Thoroughbreds were first bred around 300 years ago in England. Local riding horses and Arabians were mated to create these skilled racing and jumping horses. The United States now breeds more Thoroughbreds than any other country.

APPEARANCE

Thoroughbreds are slim but muscular horses with long legs and small hooves. They have long necks, wide chests, and short backs. They may be bay, chestnut, brown, black, or gray.

SKILLS AND TRAITS

These light horses are hardworking, energetic, and high-spirited. These qualities make them strong racing horses. Thoroughbreds can run more than 40 miles (64 kilometers) per hour. They also participate in dressage, fox hunting, and polo.

HEIGHT COMPARISON

54IN (137 cm)	64IN (163 cm)	64IN (163 cm)
standard donkey	Friesian horse	Thoroughbred horse

FAMOUS THOROUGHBRED

LEXINGTON

- **Location:** Kentucky
- **Famous for:** Lexington was a champion Thoroughbred racehorse. The horse set a world record by running 4 miles (6.4 kilometers) in just over seven minutes in 1855.

ORIGIN MAP

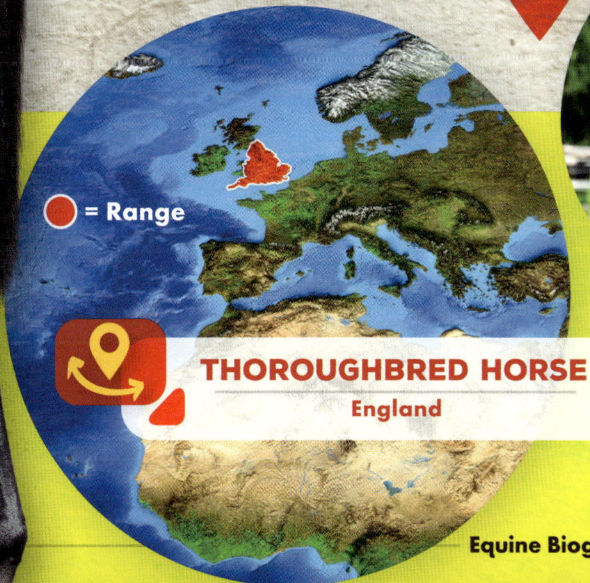

THOROUGHBRED HORSE
England

BIG STEPS

Thoroughbreds can cover 20 feet (6 meters) in one stride.

APPALOOSA HORSES

The Nez Perce people first bred Appaloosa horses in the 1700s. These horses were bred from Spanish horses. They are named after the Palouse River in the northwestern U.S.

NEZ PERCE ▼

ORIGIN MAP

SKILLS AND TRAITS

These horses are fast, loyal, and strong. They are popular for everyday riding, herding cattle, and racing. They are also skilled in Western riding events such as roping and barrel racing.

HEIGHT COMPARISON

FAVORITE HORSE

The Appaloosa is the official state horse of Idaho.

FAMOUS APPALOOSA

Zip Cochise

- **Location:** Spalding, Idaho

- **Famous for:** Zip Cochise was an Appaloosa with a brown and white coat and dark spots. The horse appeared in the 1966 classic western movie *El Dorado* starring John Wayne.

APPEARANCE

Appaloosas are compact and strong. Their coats come in shades of brown, black, gray, or white with contrasting spots. Some are spotted all over. Others have spotted patches. They often have striped hooves.

AMERICAN QUARTER HORSES

American quarter horses are light horses. They were first bred in the 1600s in the southeastern U.S.

HEIGHT COMPARISON

60IN (152 cm)
American quarter horse

60IN (152 cm)
Appaloosa horse

56IN (142 cm)
Morgan horse

SPEED RACERS

American quarter horses can run up to 55 miles (89 kilometers) per hour.

ORIGIN MAP

AMERICAN QUARTER HORSE

Virginia

SKILLS AND TRAITS

American quarter horses are calm and patient. They are often found working on ranches. Their sprinting ability shines in timed rodeo events such as roping and barrel racing. They also compete in jumping and dressage.

BARREL RACING

FAMOUS AMERICAN QUARTER HORSE

EASY JET

Location:
Sayre, Oklahoma

Famous for:
Easy Jet was one of the greatest racehorses of all time. He won 27 out of 38 races. He became the racing world champion in 1969. He was inducted into the American Quarter Horse Hall of Fame in 1993.

APPEARANCE

These horses are short and stocky with muscular upper legs. They have wide heads and chests. Their coats can be different shades of red, brown, gray, white, or black. A single white stripe often marks the face.

FRIESIAN HORSES

Friesian horses are light draft horses from Friesland in the northern Netherlands. They are descended from war horses of the Middle Ages that were crossbred with light horse breeds. They are one of the oldest domestic breeds in Europe.

▲MEDIEVAL REENACTMENT

APPEARANCE

Friesians have distinct black coats. They have large eyes and long faces. They hold their strong, arched necks high. They are known for their long manes and tails and feathered leg hair.

ORIGIN MAP

HEIGHT COMPARISON

RELATED HORSES

DESTRIERS

- **Known for:**
  Destriers were the horses of medieval knights in the Middle Ages. These strong, elegant horses were highly trained and heavily built. They were used in fighting wars and jousting.

SKILLS AND TRAITS

These horses are gentle, strong, agile, and fast. They are known for their high-stepping gait. They are a popular breed for dressage and are also used for everyday riding.

MORGAN HORSES

Morgan horses are light horses that were first bred in New England. These horses are known for their stamina and friendly nature.

ORIGIN MAP

SKILLS AND TRAITS

Morgans are athletic horses with a light, springy gait. They can pull carriages and carry riders for long distances. They are smart and eager to please. These traits make them excellent show and dressage horses.

APPEARANCE

Morgan horses have short, strong backs that are perfect for riding. They have wide foreheads, deep chests, and strong hind legs. Their coat colors vary widely, but many have brown, black, bay, or pale base colors.

FAMOUS MORGAN HORSE

FIGURE

Location:
New England

Famous for:
Figure was the original Morgan horse. He was born in 1789. He quickly became known for his speed and strength. All Morgan horses today are related to Figure.

SHIRE HORSES

Shire horses are the world's heaviest breed. These draft horses are descended from the powerful horses knights rode in medieval England.

APPEARANCE

Shire horses have long necks, sloping shoulders, and short backs. Their coats may be black, gray, or shades of brown. Some have white markings on their faces and legs. Their legs are feathered below the knee.

WHAT'S IN A NAME?

Shire horses are named after the shires, or counties, in England where they were originally used for farming and war.

ORIGIN MAP

HEIGHT COMPARISON

60IN (152 cm)

Connemara pony

60IN (152 cm)

Arabian horse

68IN (173 cm)

shire horse

FAMOUS SHIRE HORSE

SAMPSON

- **Location:** England
- **Famous for:** Sampson was born in 1846. He still holds the record for the tallest and heaviest horse ever recorded. He was 7 feet, 2 inches (2.2 meters) tall. He weighed 3,359 pounds (1,524 kilograms).

SKILLS AND TRAITS

Shire horses are gentle, hardworking, and easy to train. They once pulled cannons and farm plows over long distances. They are used today for pulling logs and farm equipment. They are also popular riding horses and horse show favorites.

CONNEMARA
PONIES

Connemara ponies are the largest pony breed. They come from the Connemara region in western Ireland. These sport ponies are excellent jumpers.

SKILLS AND TRAITS

These ponies are smart and strong. They enjoy interacting with people. Their smooth gait makes them great for riding. They pull carriages in races. They also perform show jumping and dressage.

APPEARANCE

They have long necks, strong backs, and wide chests. Their muscular hind legs help them jump and gallop. Their coats can be gray, black, or shades of brown.

ORIGIN MAP

CONNEMARA PONY
western Ireland

IRISH NATIVE

Connemara ponies are Ireland's only unique horse breed.

FAMOUS CONNEMARA

DUNDRUM

- **Location:** Ireland

- **Famous for:** Dundrum was famous for his high show jumps. He performed in many shows in the 1950s and 1960s. He jumped over walls that were around 7 feet (2.1 meters) high.

HEIGHT COMPARISON

60IN (152 cm)

Connemara pony

60IN (152 cm)

Grévy's zebra

64IN (163 cm)

Thoroughbred horse

SHETLAND PONIES

Shetland ponies have lived on the Shetland Islands off northern Scotland for more than 4,000 years. They have adapted to become a strong breed that is able to survive the rough landscape and cold climate.

ORIGIN MAP

HEIGHT COMPARISON

40IN (102 cm)

Shetland pony

54IN (137 cm)

standard donkey

52IN (132 cm)

Przewalski's horse

SKILLS AND TRAITS

Shetland ponies are smart and playful. They were once used for hauling heavy loads. Today, these ponies are mostly kept as pets and for children to ride. They also pull carriages, race, and perform in horse shows.

APPEARANCE

These small ponies have short, muscular necks and legs. They have straight, thick manes and tails.

FAMOUS SHETLAND

TEDDY

- **Location:**
  England

- **Famous for:**
  Teddy the Shetland is a therapy pony who visits hospitals and nursing homes. He cheers people up with his sweet and gentle nature. He has more than 180,000 followers on Instagram.

AMERICAN MUSTANG HORSES

American mustangs are feral horses. They are descended from domestic Spanish horses that came to the Americas in the 1500s. Modern mustangs are a mix of several breeds.

APPEARANCE

They have strong backs, wide foreheads, and narrow chests. Their straight legs and thick hooves give them a smooth gait. They can be white, black, or many shades of brown. Some have spotted patches.

SKILLS AND TRAITS

American mustangs are strong horses with feet adapted to rough terrain and traveling long distances. They travel in groups called harems. These include a single stallion that protects several mares and foals. Bachelor groups contain only young stallions.

HEIGHT COMPARISON

52IN (132 cm)	60IN (152 cm)	56IN (142 cm)
Przewalski's horse	Appaloosa horse	American mustang

VULNERABLE SPECIES

▼ AMERICAN MUSTANG ▼

THREAT

confinement in holding areas when population is too high in a region

CONSERVATION EFFORTS ▼

- population management
- laws that protect the horses and their habitats
- adoption programs

PRZEWALSKI'S HORSES

Przewalski's horses are the only true wild horses in the world. These horses once lived throughout Europe and Asia. Today, small numbers live in Mongolia and China.

SKILLS AND TRAITS

Przewalski's horses live in harems. Stallions leave their droppings on top of mare droppings from their harem. This keeps other stallions away.

VULNERABLE SPECIES

▼ PRZEWALSKI'S HORSE ▼
ENDANGERED

THREAT

small population due to low breeding rates and past threats such as hunting and wars

CONSERVATION EFFORTS ▼

- **cloning**
- **release into the wild for natural breeding**

HEIGHT COMPARISON

52IN (132 cm)	56IN (142 cm)	64IN (163 cm)
Przewalski's horse	Morgan horse	Friesian horse

APPEARANCE

These horses have big heads, stocky bodies, and short legs. They are sandy brown or reddish brown with white on their faces and bellies. They have dark tails and dark, short manes.

DONKEYS

Donkeys are domestic equines. They are descended from the African wild ass. Donkeys are often grouped by size instead of breed. The three sizes are miniature, standard, and mammoth.

▼ MINIATURE DONKEYS

◀ MAMMOTH DONKEY

APPEARANCE

Donkey coats are often black, white, or gray. They often have dark stripes on their backs and shoulders. Their heads are large, and their ears are long. They have short, thick manes.

ORIGIN MAP

HINNY

MULE

SKILLS AND TRAITS

Donkeys are very smart. They have strong memories and take time to make safe decisions in difficult situations. Common jobs include farmwork and keeping predators away from livestock.

MINIATURE DONKEYS

Miniature donkeys are the smallest donkeys. They can grow to about 36 inches (91 centimeters) tall. That is about the length of a baseball bat.

SPECIES PROFILE

HYBRIDS

- **Names:** mules and hinnies
- **Known for:** A mule is a cross between a male donkey and a female horse. A hinny is the offspring of a stallion and a female donkey. Mules and hinnies cannot produce young.

HEIGHT COMPARISON

60IN (152 cm)

Connemara pony

54IN (137 cm)

standard donkey

60IN (152 cm)

Arabian horse

ZEBRAS

Zebras are wild equines. Mountain zebras roam the rocky hills of Angola, Namibia, and South Africa. Grévy's zebras live in the grasslands of Kenya and Ethiopia. Plains zebras roam grasslands in eastern and southern Africa.

▲ MOUNTAIN ZEBRAS

APPEARANCE

Zebras have black-and-white stripes that vary in size and spacing. They have big heads, striped manes, long legs, and tasseled tails. A stripe runs along their spines.

▼ GRÉVY'S ZEBRAS

SKILLS AND TRAITS

Zebras are social and playful herd animals. They have strong hearing and eyesight. Their speed and powerful kicks help keep them safe from lions and hyenas.

HEIGHT COMPARISON

52IN (132 cm)

Przewalski's horse

60IN (152 cm)

Grévy's zebra

60IN (152 cm)

American quarter horse

SPECIES PROFILE

GRANT'S ZEBRA

- **Location:** eastern and southeastern Africa
- **Known for:** Grant's zebras are a subspecies of plains zebras. They are known for their migration during the rainy season in the Serengeti. They often travel in groups of 10,000.

EQUINES AND PEOPLE

Domesticating horses made it possible for many civilizations to survive and grow. Horses have been important in travel, trade, and war. Many cultures have honored equines for their strength, beauty, and loyalty. Equines are often shown in art, books, and movies.

Domestic and wild horses often face threats caused by human behaviors. Some horses are purposely hurt or given medicines to make them run faster or perform better in shows. These practices are only done for people's entertainment. Hunting, habitat loss, and climate change threaten wild and feral equines.

FOLKLORE PROFILE

NAME:

PEGASUS

COUNTRY:

GREECE

FAMOUS FOR:

Pegasus is a mythological horse with white wings. He inspired creativity, helped gods in difficult situations, and brought thunderbolts to Zeus. He was awarded for his good efforts by being turned into a constellation.

Many organizations and laws work to keep domestic equines safe. Education programs help people take better care of these animals. The Horse Protection Act keeps horses safe from harmful practices.

▼ HORSE CONSERVATION AREA

Wild and feral equines are protected too. Laws protect their habitats. They ban hunting, injuring, and removing these animals from their natural homes. Conservation sites also take care of these equines.

PRZEWALSKI'S HORSE CONSERVATIONISTS

People can help equines by supporting conservation programs. They can encourage governments to pass more laws to fight climate change and habitat destruction. By working together, these animals can live safely for many more years to come!

MUSTANG PROTECTED LAND

GLOSSARY

adapted—changed over a period of time

ancestors—relatives who lived long ago

Berber—related to people who are originally from northwestern Africa

breeds—types of domestic horses

civilizations—communities with set ways of life

climate—the usual temperature, precipitation, and other weather conditions of an area

climate change—a human-caused process in which Earth's average weather changes over a long period of time

conservation sites—land areas that are protected and cannot be built on or used for certain purposes

crossbred—produced by breeding two different breeds of horses

cultures—the beliefs, arts, and ways of life in a place or society

descended—came from an animal that lived at an earlier time

domestic—related to living near or around human settlements

dressage—a horse show event judged on movement, balance, and the ability to follow directions

equids—mammals in the family Equidae that include horses, donkeys, zebras, and extinct related animals

evolved—changed from one form into a new form

feathered—having longer hair

feral—related to horses that have escaped from domestication and become wild

gait—a way of walking

habitats—natural homes of plants and animals

harems—groups of female horses that include one male

mammals—warm-blooded animals that have backbones and feed their young milk

Middle Ages—a period of European history from about 500 to 1500

migrated—moved from one place to another

peninsula—a section of land that sticks out from a larger piece of land and is almost completely surrounded by water

species—groups of living things that are alike and can reproduce with one another; subspecies are particular types of animals that exist within a species.

stamina—the ability to run for a long time

subtropical—related to areas bordering the tropics; the tropics is a hot, rainy region near the equator.

threats—behaviors that cause harm

traits—qualities that make one horse different from others

WRITE ABOUT IT!

- What species of equines would you like to learn more about? **Why?**
- What equine behavior do you think is the most interesting? **Why?**
- **What** changes can you make in your life that could help keep equines and their habitats safe?

ALSO CHECK OUT

INDEX

The images in this book are reproduced through the courtesy of: Osetrik, front cover, p. 1; lee, front cover, p. 1; Quality Stock Arts, front cover, p. 1; Rita Kochmarjova, front cover, pp. 1, 14 (top), 21 (left), 32 (top, middle, main), 33 (right); Hanna, front cover, p. 1; abubakar0023, front cover, p. 1; Dan, pp. 3, 38; Lily, p. 3; callipso88, p. 4 (top); belyaaa, p. 4 (left); christy, p. 4 (right); Sunshine Seeds, p. 4 (bottom); Magnus, p. 4 (mane); Alexey Stiop, p. 4; Heinrich Harder/ Wikimedia Commons, p. 6 (top, middle); LRBurdak/ Wikimedia Commons, p. 6 (bottom); Tetiana Yurkovska, pp. 7 (top), 28 (left); alesmunt, p. 7 (left); Olga Itina, pp. 7 (right), 16, 17 (main), 21, 24, 25 (main); pfluegler photo, p. 8 (top); kathomenden, pp. 8 (left), 24 (top); Gunter Nuyts, p. 8 (right); Kateryna Kalynovska, p. 8 (bottom); George Dolgikh, p. 9; Lorena, p. 9 (horse); ccestep8, p. 9 (donkey); fishcat007, p. 9 (zebra); Ivan, p. 9 (bottom); adipictures, p. 10 (top); Laura Kezbere, p. 10 (middle); Raeann Davies, p. 10 (bottom); Geza Farkas, p. 11 (top); Marie Charouzova, p. 11 (left); Composer, p. 11 (right); Angela N Perryman, p. 11 (bottom); Mark J. Barrett, pp. 12 (shire), 24 (right); stonefly, p. 12 (thoroughbred); lenkadan, pp. 12 (quarter), 16 (top); Yerbolat, pp. 12 (przewalski's), 36 (bottom); Bob Pool, pp. 12 (mustang), 42 (bottom); Rita_Kochmarjova, pp. 13 (Shetland), 14, 15 (main), 20; nigel baker photography, p. 13 (Connemara); tr3gi, p. 13 (zebra); DragoNika, p. 13 (donkey); markup, p. 14 (middle); Dr Ajay Kumar Singh, p. 14 (bottom); Reimar, p. 15 (top); Hercules Milas/ Alamy Stock Photo, p. 15 (profile); slowmotiongli, pp. 15, 21 (bottom), 31 (top), 40 (grévy's); Babalola, p. 16; rima15, pp. 16 (bottom), 27 (left); Sotheby's/ Wikimedia Commons, p. 17 (profile); Azahara, p. 17 (left); Dmytro Cherniavskyi, p. 17 (right); Gaertner/ Alamy Stock Photo, p. 18 (top); Sushchina Marya, p. 18 (middle); encierro, pp. 18, 19; PicMedia, p. 18 (bottom); geptays, pp. 18, 19 (main); James Mullen/ Wikimedia Commons, p. 19 (profile); Alexander_fotolab, p. 19 (bottom); YellowstoneNPS/ Wikimedia Commons, p. 20 (top); NA/ Wikimedia Commons, p. 21 (profile); NA, p. 21 (top); Julia Remezova, p. 21 (right); Christy berry, p. 22 (top); www.MartinaBurianova.cz, p. 22 (left); Ehoggard/ Wirestock Creators, p. 22 (right); Robiny, p. 23; Sabine Hagedorn, p. 23 (bottom); Walt Wiggins/ Wikimedia Commons, p. 23 (profile); Debra Angel, p. 24; horsemen, pp. 24 (left), 28 (right); Viktoria Makarova, p. 25 (top); ppolecho, p. 25 (middle); Matthew Paris/ Wikimedia Commons, p. 25 (profile); vprotastchik, p. 25 (bottom); Christopher Crosby Morris, p. 26 (top); Shawn Hamilton CLiX, p. 26 (left); Joy Brown, p. 26 (right); Jackie Warinner, p. 26 (bottom); Horse Crazy, p. 27 (top); Kirk, p. 27 (right); Lisa Kolbenschlag, p. 27 (main); Sophie Callahan/ Wirestock, p. 28 (bottom); Eric Isselée, pp. 28 (main), 33, 38; Jenny Thompson, p. 29 (top); paula, p. 29; Louis-Michel DESERT, p. 30 (top); Juniors Bildarchiv GmbH/ Alamy Stock Photo, p. 30 (left); rapha064, p. 30 (right); agephotography, p. 30 (bottom); Patryk Kosmider, p. 30 (main); Bildagentur Zoonar GmbH, p. 31; Split Seconds/ Alamy Stock Photo, p. 31 (profile); Alan, p. 32 (bottom); cynoclub, p. 33 (top); Pelana, p. 33 (left); Ivana, p. 34 (top); gchapel, p. 34 (middle); Gian Sapienza Photography, p. 34 (bottom); Mikhail Gnatkovskiy/ Alamy Stock Photo, p. 34; natureguy, p. 35 (top); John Boland, p. 35 (left); Danita Delimont/ Alamy Stock Photo, p. 35 (right); PhotocechCZ, p. 36 (top); Vlasto Opatovsky, p. 36 (middle); Kamil Kubalik, p. 36 (left); ene_A, p. 36 (right); Staffan Widstrand, p. 37 (top); Michar Peppenster, p. 37 (middle); Valerii Kaliuzhnyi, p. 37 (main); Peter Oetelshofen, p. 37 (bottom); equigini, p. 38 (top); Tracy Kerestesh, p. 38 (middle); mexitographer, p. 38 (bottom); Sirisak_baokaew, p. 39 (hinny); Julia Kuznetsova, p. 39 (top); Martin, p. 39 (middle); Sonja Birkelbach, p. 39 (bottom); Christopher J Barger, p. 39 (mule); JMx Images, p. 40 (top); gudkovandrey, p. 40 (middle); Jandrie Lombard, p. 40 (left); Tyrone, p. 40 (right); Evans, p. 40; Tau5, p. 41 (top); Rixie, p. 41; Hans Hillewaert/ Wikimedia Commons, p. 41 (profile); The Cesnola Collection/ Wikimedia Commons, p. 42 (left); Gift of Henry Hilton/ Wikimedia Commons, p. 42 (middle); Sharon Hahn Darlin/ Wikimedia Commons, p. 42 (right); Pic Media Aus, p. 43 (left); kat7213, p. 43 (right); Jan Boeckhorst/ Wikimedia Commons, p. 43 (middle); Johann Bayer/ Wikimedia Commons, p. 43 (bottom); Edwin Remsberg/ Alamy Stock Photo, p. 44 (top); Jack Bell Photography, p. 44; Arend de Haas/ Alamy Stock Photo, p. 44 (bottom); Xinhua News Agency/ Getty Images, p. 45 (top); Tom Tietz, p. 45 (middle); Marigold, p. 45 (left); olodymyr Burdiak, p. 45 (right).